W9-BNU-827

DATE			

⌐/97

STAGE
2

WHAT COLOR IS
CAMOUFLAGE?

by Carolyn Otto

illustrated by Megan Lloyd

HarperCollinsPublishers

The illustrations in this book were done with watercolor and pen and ink
on Saunders Waterford Watercolor Paper.

The *Let's-Read-and-Find-Out Science* book series was originated by Dr. Franklyn M. Branley, Astronomer Emeritus
and former Chairman of the American Museum–Hayden Planetarium, and was formerly co-edited by him and
Dr. Roma Gans, Professor Emeritus of Childhood Education, Teachers College, Columbia University. Text and illustrations for each of the books in the series are checked for accuracy by an expert in the relevant field. For more infor-
mation about the Let's-Read-and-Find-Out Science books, write to HarperCollins Children's Books, 10 East 53rd
Street, New York, NY 10022.

HarperCollins®, ☕®, and Let's Read-and-Find-Out Science® are trademarks of HarperCollins Publishers Inc.

Library of Congress Cataloging-in-Publication Data
Otto, Carolyn.
    What color is camouflage? / by Carolyn Otto ; illustrated by Megan
Lloyd.
        p.   cm. — (Let's-read-and-find-out science. Stage 1)
    Summary: Explains how animal markings and colorings vary in
response to their environment.
        ISBN 0-06-027094-2. — ISBN 0-06-027099-3 (lib. bdg.)
        ISBN 0-06-445160-7 (pbk.)
    1. Camouflage (Biology)—Juvenile literature. [1.Camouflage
(Biology).   2. Animal defenses.]   I. Lloyd, Megan, ill.   II. Title.
III. Series.
QL767.077   1996   95-32173
591.57'2—dc20   CIP
                                                            AC

Typography by Al Cetta
1   2   3   4   5   6   7   8   9   10
❖
First Edition

WHAT COLOR IS
CAMOUFLAGE?

Mountain Lion

4

Mule Deer

In the foothills near my house, a mountain lion might be hunting. He stalks across a dry hillside. His golden fur matches the grass.

A doe raises her head to sniff the air. Her fawn is quiet, and the lion passes by.

In my backyard, a robin could catch an insect that looks like a leaf.

American Robin

6

Striped Skunks

After dark, a skunk and her babies might walk right down my street. My dog can see their bold white stripes, but he's learned to leave skunks alone.

Near my house, and all over the world, at
every time of day or night, animals are hunting
for food . . . or they are being hunted.

Field Mice

Bobca

Animals must eat in order to live, and to live they sometimes have to hide. Animals hide in holes, burrows, and dens, in plants, underwater, and beneath rocks.

Great Horned Owl

Yellow-Bellied Marmots

Short-Horned Lizard

9

Mountain
Lion

Mule Deer

Some animals hide out in plain sight, but they
are still very hard to see. The doe's coat and the
mountain lion's fur blend into the colors
surrounding them.

The fawn's spots match the sun and shade that dapple the thicket where she hides. When in danger, the fawn must stay very still. Any movement might draw the eye of a hunter.

The fawn and the doe, and the prowling lion— each one of these animals is camouflaged.

Mule Deer Fawn

What color is camouflage? Camouflage can be a certain color, or pattern of colors, or a special shape that fools the eye. Animal camouflage is a kind of disguise. It makes an animal hard to see.

Camouflage helps an animal hide from enemies, and it can help a hunter sneak up on its prey.

Red Fox

Eastern Chipmunks

Hiding and hunting are both made easier when an animal matches its surroundings. A green insect clinging to a green leaf is much harder to see than a red insect. If a green insect is shaped like a leaf, even the hungriest bird could miss it.

Stinkbugs

Spotted Asparagus Beetles

Scarlet-and-Green Leafhoppers

Hermit Crab

Some animals disguise themselves by dressing in plants, pebbles, even other living things. Many crabs are experts at decorating their bodies with seaweed, shells, rocks, sponges, or anemones.

Lesser Sponge Crab

Stick Insect

Red Bat

When animals are perfectly camouflaged,
sticks seem to crawl, leaves can fly, and a stone
may have eyes and a beak.

Common Poorwill

15

High up in the mountains above my house, this rock-colored ptarmigan warms her eggs. In summer, a ptarmigan has many dark feathers. By snowfall, her feathers will be pure white.

White-Tailed Jackrabbit

White-Tailed Ptarmigan

When the surrounding world changes color,
certain animals can change right along. Some,
like the ptarmigan, change slowly. Her feathers
change color as she molts.

Only the dark eyes and tips of his ears give
away a jackrabbit in his winter coat.

Young animals may change coloring as they
grow —as they get big, or strong, or very swift.

Mule Deer

The fawn's spots will gradually fade, when she can run away from danger.

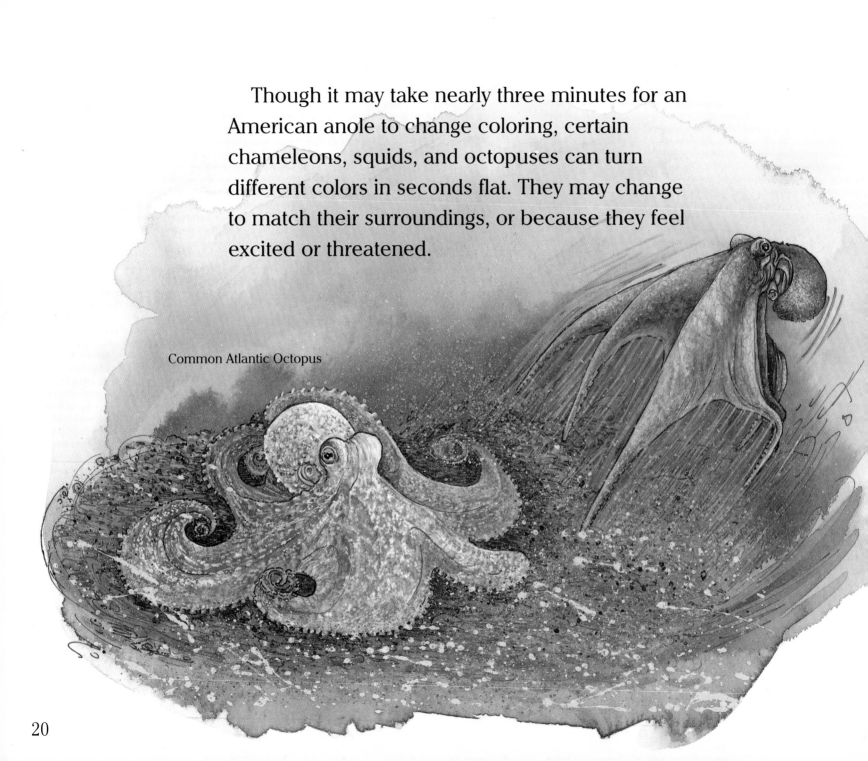

Though it may take nearly three minutes for an American anole to change coloring, certain chameleons, squids, and octopuses can turn different colors in seconds flat. They may change to match their surroundings, or because they feel excited or threatened.

Common Atlantic Octopus

Green Anoles

21

American Robins

Many animals don't ever change. Some don't
need any camouflage. These animals don't have
to hide. Their colors may attract attention.

A robin's red breast helps him find a mate, and
a skunk's bold stripes are a warning.

Animals sometimes use colors or bright
patterns to say:

"I smell,"

Spotted Skunk

"I sting,"

Yellow Jacket

or "I'm poisonous."

Gila Monster

Once sprayed by a skunk or stung by a bee, a hunter learns to avoid them next time.

Bobcat

Spotted Skunk

Honey Bee

Hover Fly

Arizona Coral Snake

Organ Pipe Shovel-Nosed Snake

Eastern Newt

Red Salamander

Harmless animals may copy warning signals to
protect themselves from their enemies.

Black Swallowtail

A flash of bright color may be enough to fool a predator, or to scare it away. Some animals have spots that look like eyes. Eyespots can frighten or confuse an enemy. A hunter may strike at "eyes" on a wing or tail, which gives the prey a small chance to escape.

Buckeye

Common Toad

Gray Treefrog

Green Lacewing

Praying Mantis

Whether hunter or hunted, predator or prey,
colors and camouflage help an animal survive.

Queen Hornet Wasp

Wherever you live, animals live near you.

In backyards and in city parks, outside and inside your house, in plants, underwater, in air, animals are everywhere.

Do you see an animal?

An animal you can spot right away may be saying something important.

Black Widow Spider

read and discuss
the rest of the
book

28

Pine
Grosbeak

Spotted Skunk

29

Look closely, and more closely still. Look at colors, patterns, and shapes:

an old stump could be a bird,

a green branch may be a snake,

a twig might be a caterpillar,

a thorn might be an insect,

a rock may be a turtle,

and a dead leaf could be a toad.

Look closely when you go outside. Can you find the hidden animals?

Oak Inchworm Catterpillar

Smooth Green Snake

Flammulated
Owl

Snapping Turtle

Western Toad

Buffalo Treehopper

31

When animals are camouflaged, they can be
very hard to see.